Straight Answers to Tough Questions

20 Quick Answers for Creationists' Defense of the Christian Faith

by Dr. John Morris & Doug Phillips, Esq.

Straight Answers to Tough Questions
Formerly titled: *Weapons of Our Warfare*
by John D. Morris, Ph.D., & Doug Phillips, Esq.

Copyright © 1998, 2002

Institute for Creation Research
P.O. Box 2667
El Cajon, CA 92021-0667

ISBN #0-932766-80-3

Editor: Mark Rasche
Assistant Editor: Ruth Richards
Cover Design: Creative Imagery & Design

Printed in the United States of America

Topical Index

Introduction 5

Age of the Earth 6
How Old Is the Earth, According to the Bible?

Creation and the Church 8
Should a Church Take a Stand on Creation?

Creation, Belief in 10
Why Should a Christian Believe in Creation?

Creation Ministry, Purpose of 12
What Is the Purpose of the Creation Ministry?

Dinosaurs 14
How Do the Dinosaurs Fit In?

Evidence against Evolution 16
Is There Evidence Against Evolution?

Family 18
A Genesis Solution for America's Failing Families?

Fossils, Human 20
Why Don't We Find More Human Fossils?

Geologic Column, The 22
Does the Geologic Column Prove Evolution?

Ice Age, The 24
Was There Really an Ice Age?

Law and Evolution 26
Do Laws and Standards Evolve?

Macroevolution vs. Microevolution 28
What's the Difference Between Macro- and Microevolution?

Noah's Flood 30
Did Noah's Flood Cover the Whole Earth?

Public Schools, Evolution in the 32
Are Public Schools Required to Teach Evolution?

Questions, Ten Most Asked 34
Do the Difficult Questions Have Answers?

Races, The 36
Where Did the Races Come From?

Radioisotope Dating 38
Can Radioisotope Dating Be Trusted?

Theories 40
Can Evolution Be Harmonized with Genesis?

Theistic Evolution 42
Is the God of Theistic Evolution the Same as the God of the Bible?

Young Earth, Belief in the 44
Is Belief in the Young Earth Necessary to Be a Christian?

Key Bible Verses on Creation 46

Creation thinking has been around for a long time, yet it is strangely obscure in many Christian circles today. Intimidated by scientists claiming more knowledge than they really have, many Christians have retreated on this foundational issue.

Many of our leading evangelical liberal arts colleges and seminaries teach theistic evolution, billions of years of history, local flood, an allegorical Genesis, or some other accommodation to the naturalistic worldview.

Unfortunately, the issue does not stop with the various ideas about history. The false worldview of evolution (and its evangelical stepsisters) has led millions into wrong life-style decisions reeking untold havoc worldwide. Evolution, as the basis for Marxism, Fascism, Freudian psychology, racism, etc., has been well documented, but modern ills such as homosexual behavior, abortion, promiscuity, radical feminism, and many others, likewise look to evolution for intellectual justification. Wrong thinking always begets wrong behavior.

Thus there is the need for a "Back to Genesis" way of thinking. Christians need to base all their thinking, in every area, on the teachings of Scripture and the foundation of Scripture is Genesis. In Genesis, we learn the identity of God, the nature of man, the consequences of sin—concepts without which we cannot know eternal life. In Genesis we also learn of God's design for His creation—without which we cannot experience right living today.

How can we go "Back to Genesis," especially when our thinking has been so clouded by wrong teaching? Renewing our minds in submission to God's truth may not be easy and will take a lifetime, but Christians must endorse the Biblical worldview.

This booklet is designed to help. Laid out in question and answer format, it provides answers to some of the most common questions and ideas for implementation of these answers. Most importantly, it provides examples of how to think—how to recognize error, discern truth, and apply right thinking in our lives. With this as an aide, we can begin to go "Back to Genesis" for a God-pleasing and fruitful walk with Him.

Age of the Earth

How Old Is the Earth, According to the Bible?

The Institute for Creation Research has always taught, as an integral part of its ministry, the concept of a young earth. We have never put an absolute date on the age of the earth. We feel that the Bible doesn't provide all the information necessary for certainty, as shown by the fact that almost every Bible scholar who has ever tried to discern the exact date has come to slightly different conclusions. Maybe all the information is there, but we just don't understand it fully yet.

However, lest we be too concerned, every honest attempt to determine the date, starting with a deep commitment to the inerrancy of God's word, has calculated a span of just a few thousand years, most likely close to 6,000 years, since creation. The largest figure I've ever seen from a trustworthy scholar is approximately 15,000 years, but even this seems to stretch the Biblical data too far.

To calculate the date, one must first employ the genealogical data given in Genesis, I and II Chronicles, the Gospels, and elsewhere. Information gleaned from Judges, I and II Kings, Daniel, Acts, and other books must be included as well. Since dates are fairly well established archaeologically beginning at about the time of David, these can be a big help. This is because so many Biblical events are referenced to the reigns of individual kings. Obviously, the job is difficult.

Of course the genealogies only begin with the creation of Adam, so the question of time before Adam remains. As has been well noted in ICR literature, the six days of Creation Week must be of the same length as our days. We recognize, however, that the Hebrew word *yom*, translated "day," can have a variety of meanings, including an indefinite period of time. Thus, some have suggested that these six days might then be equated with the billions of years claimed by geologists.

Whenever a word in Scripture can have a variety of meanings, we must go to the context to determine what it *does* mean in a particular case, and not be content with what it *might* mean. And when we do, we find that the first time *yom* is used (Genesis 1:5), it is a solar day (v. 3) and described as a total day/night cycle. Furthermore, *yom* is modified by "evening and morning," which, in Hebrew, can only mean a literal day. It is also modified by an ordinal number (first, second, etc.), a construction limited in Hebrew to that of a literal day.

Elsewhere, the six days of creation are equated with the six days of our work week (Exodus 20:11), a formula incorporated in the fourth of the Ten Commandments regarding the Sabbath rest. We should mention that the use of a numeral to modify "days," in this case "six," is again reserved for a literal day in Hebrew, as is the use of the plural word "days."

Suffice it to say that no literalist could rightly conclude that Scripture specifically places Creation any longer ago than a few thousand years, and to my knowledge no one does. Many do hold to an older position, but not for Scriptural reasons. They are convinced by radioisotope dating, perhaps, or maybe the molecular clock of mutation rates, or some other line of thinking, but not from Scripture. (These and other dating techniques are all scientifically flawed. They are discussed elsewhere.)

Scripture teaches a young earth, and the time has come for Christians to stop twisting Scripture to fit the evolutionary and uniformitarian speculations of some scientists about the unobserved past. We suggest it's time for such Christians to stop calling themselves "Bible-believing" Christians and start using some such name as "world-believing" Christians, for they clearly place more credence in the words of fallible men than in the words of the infallible God.

Recommended Resources:
The Young Earth—J. Morris
The Genesis Record—H. Morris
The Young Age of the Earth (video)—H. Morris
A Geological Perspective on the Age of the Earth (video)—J. Morris

Creation and the Church

Should a Church Take a Stand on Creation?

Recently my family and I (John D. Morris) joined a small church pastored by a former student of mine at Christian Heritage College—a man of real wisdom and integrity.

A church constitution was being written, which, of course, included a Statement of Faith. A solid creation and young-earth plank appeared in the first draft.

Although there was no disagreement among the members (many of whom were young Christians) as to the doctrine of special recent creation, there was concern in making this a requirement for membership. I was asked to comment.

Given the fact that most of America's Bible colleges and seminaries would not even agree with the content of the plank, I acknowledged my own hesitancy about being so exclusive, but in a series of Sunday evening messages, I demonstrated how beliefs in creation and a young earth are integral parts of Christianity.

First, the doctrine of God's character is at stake. For example: Is the God of the Bible a gracious, purposeful God of wisdom, or does He resort to trial and error in His deeds, testing His creation by survival of the fittest and delighting in the extinction of the weaker? Is God long ago and far away—only occasionally involved, or is He near and intimately concerned with the affairs of life?

The doctrine of Scripture comes into play. There are few Biblical teachings as clear as that of creation in six days and the companion doctrine of the global flood. Yet these two teachings are denied and ridiculed in many "Bible-believing" churches today. Can the Scriptures be trusted? Can God say what He means? If one who claims to be a Christian leader or teacher can distort Scripture to teach such beliefs as evolution, progressive creation, an old earth, or a local flood, can that Christian be trusted with other doctrines?

Without creation, the doctrine of man becomes skewed. Can man, with a brain and reasoning powers distorted by the curse, evaluating only a portion of the evidence, accurately reconstruct the history of the universe? Should his historical reconstructions be put on a higher plane than Scripture? Or is man and his mind locked in the effects of the curse—an incomplete reflection of the once-glorious "image of God"—now blinded by sin and the god of this world, seeing things "through a glass darkly"?

If evolution and old-earth thinking are incorporated, the doctrine of sin becomes questionable as well. If death and bloodshed preceded Adam's rebellion against God, then what are "the wages of sin"? How did the entrance of sin change things?

The doctrine of salvation likewise falls, for if death preceded sin, then death is not the penalty for sin, and Christ's death on the cross accomplished nothing. Any form of evolution and old-earth thinking is incompatible with the work of Christ.

My conclusion surprised some in the congregation. Young-earth creationism should not be a requirement for church membership since new members would include new Christians as well as Christians who have been wrongly taught, and it would only be proper to give new members time to grow and mature under good teaching. A church constitution is a "here we stand" document, and not a series of hoops to jump through to be associated.

But I do know one thing: Creationism should be a requirement for Christian leadership! No church should sanction a pastor, Sunday school teacher, deacon, elder, or Bible-study leader who knowledgeably and purposefully errs on this crucial doctrine, for all other doctrines find their foundation in this one.

Recommended Resources:

The Defender's Study Bible—H. Morris
The Lie: Evolution—Ham
Genesis and the Decay of the Nations—Ham
The Young Age of the Earth (video)—H. Morris
Evolution and the Wages of Sin (video)—J. Morris

Belief in Creation

Why Should a Christian Believe in Creation?

The Institute for Creation Research is a multifaceted organization. ICR conducts meetings for university students as well as pre-schoolers. We do scientific research and speak in churches. Our goal is to produce material on every subject at every level. But perhaps the aspect that thrills us most is to see Christians come back to a belief in all of God's word, have their questions answered, and get the monkey of evolution off their backs.

There are many reasons why a Christian should be a Bible-believing creationist and not try to include any form of evolution in his thinking. In this short space, let us briefly mention several of them:

First, evolution is bad science. Anyone familiar with ICR and its materials is aware that the scientific evidence does not support evolution. Evolution is a non-testable concept, non-falsifiable, and therefore not even a proper scientific theory. It violates the basic laws of science and probability. There is no hint in the fossil record that any basic category of plant or animal has ever changed into any other. It ascribes incredibly complex life forms to pure chance.

Furthermore, evolution has evil fruits. The failed concepts of racism, fascism, Marxism, imperialism, etc., are all founded on evolutionary principles, as are the extant concepts of Freudianism, promiscuity, abortion, homosexuality, drug use, etc.

One's self-concept is tied up in his view of origins. It makes a big difference if we were created in the image of God, to bring Him glory and do His bidding, versus being the chance by-product of primeval slime.

One's entire worldview is likewise at stake. Are we here as God's stewards of life and the earth with the ministry of pointing mankind back to Him, or are we the mere products of nature, with only personal satisfaction, survival, and reproduction of importance to us as evolution teaches?

The Christian should also recognize that evolution is bad Scripture. Belief in long-age evolution requires twisting of Scriptural references in Genesis 1, Exodus 20:11, Psalm 19:1, Romans 1:20, Romans 8:20–22, Colossians 1:15–20, Hebrews 11:3, II Peter 3:3–6, etc.

Because it doesn't match with Scripture, evolution is bad theology. If evolution is true, then death preceded sin and cannot be its penalty; and, therefore, Christ's death did not pay that penalty. One's view of God is distorted when viewed through evolutionary glasses. The concept of billions of years of evolutionary meandering and extinction is inconsistent with God's omnipotence, omniscience, purposiveness, loving nature, and even His grace.

Lastly, one's personal relationship to God is related to origins. The Bible teaches us to worship God for His creative majesty (Revelation 4:11, etc.). Our prayers are enhanced as we praise Him for His creative majesty and sovereign control of our lives and all of creation. Our life's work should be to fulfill God's purpose in creation, for we were created as beings on whom He could shower His love and grace and respond to Him in reciprocal love and obedient service.

Let us not neglect to acknowledge Him as Creator, author of Scripture, and King of our lives and thoughts.

Recommended Resources:
Biblical Creationism—H. Morris
Creation and the Second Coming—H. Morris
The God Who Is Real—H. Morris
Natural Selection vs. Supernatural Design (video)—J. Morris
The Seven Days of Creation (audio tapes)—H. Morris

Purpose of Creation Ministry

What Is the Purpose of the Creation Ministry?

ICR is well known as a creation-science research group with an additional emphasis in Biblical apologetics. But first and foremost, ICR is a Christian ministry. So what are our goals?

ICR's threefold ministry of research, education, and publication is summed up in the mission statement of the ICR Graduate School: ". . . to discover and transmit the truth about the universe by scientific research and study, and to correlate and apply such scientific data within the supplemental integrating framework of Biblical creationism."

These goals reflect two Scriptural missions. One is the Great Commission given to all Christians. "Go ye therefore, and teach all nations, baptizing them. . . . Teaching them to observe all things whatsoever I have commanded you" (Matthew 28:19,20).

This commission incorporates evangelism and discipleship—the process of bringing lost individuals to a saving knowledge of Jesus Christ and helping them grow in their faith to a place of maturity and effective ministry. At ICR, God has equipped us in the area of science, and that is the tool we use to carry out our portion of the Great Commission.

In many ways, evolution has become a major barrier to evangelism. If evolution is true, then the Bible is not true. We are the product of randomly operating natural processes, and God is not necessary. Before the gospel seed can take root, the rubble of evolution must be cleared away and the ground prepared. For many confused products of our educational system, legitimate questions must be answered before a person can come to faith. Some have called creation ministry "the cutting edge of evangelism," and ICR outreaches (books, seminars, teaching) carry creation information to those in need.

But then a Christian must grow to maturity. Without doubt, evolutionary teaching hinders Christian growth. Evolution teaches that the Bible has errors and cannot be trusted. Christians need to have their questions answered and doubts removed.

Churches, seminaries, and denominations need to be called back to a belief in all of Scripture and to come under the authority of the Book they have been taught to doubt. This is the real message of creation.

An even larger commission was once given to all of mankind—the Dominion Mandate. "God said, Let us make man in our image, after our likeness: and let them have dominion over [the animals] . . . and over all the earth, . . . and subdue it" (Genesis 1:26,28). Bible believers have long understood this as a mandate to study the creation (science), and then to use it wisely for man's good and God's glory (technology). Mankind was given stewardship over creation, to care for it in wisdom as the Creator's representative on Earth.

ICR desires to follow this mission as well. Its basic research strives to answer questions, but also to more fully understand God's creative handiwork.

With the rise of evolution and naturalism, "science" has become the enemy of Christianity, but true science "declare(s) the glory of God" (Psalm 19:1). ICR desires to return science to its proper, God-glorifying position.

Recommended Resources:
The God Who Is Real—H. Morris
The Bible Has the Answer—H. Morris
The God Who Is Real (video)—H. Morris
Creation Evangelism (video)—Ham
A Walk through History (video)—J. Morris

Dinosaurs

How Do the Dinosaurs Fit In?

When first exposed to the creation model of Earth history, Christians and non-Christians alike usually ask the same question: "What about the dinosaurs?" It seems that decades of evolutionary brainwashing have led many people to equate dinosaurs with evolution. Even though dinosaurs have long been an effective tool for teaching evolutionary dogma, they really did exist, and, therefore, must somehow fit into the Biblical framework.

The Bible says that all things were created during the six-day Creation Week (Exodus 20:11, etc.), including dinosaurs. The reptilian dinosaurs were (by definition) land animals which were created on Day Six, presumably under the category of "beast of the earth" (Genesis 1:24,25). There were also large marine reptiles created on Day Five (v.21). Along with all animals and mankind, they were created to be plant eaters (vv.29,30), for there was no death before Adam and Eve rebelled against God.

Of the many dinosaur fossils found, almost all give evidence of being plant eaters exclusively. Several of the dinosaur fossil types, however, do possess sharp teeth, sharp claws, spikes, armor plates, etc., perhaps used for a variety of offensive or defensive purposes. Of course, scientists can never be certain about a creature's habits when they only have bits of dead bones to study, and most dinosaur fossils are extremely fragmentary, usually consisting of part of a single bone. And many animals alive today that have sharp teeth use them for strictly peaceful ends. But enough is known of dinosaurs to strongly suspect that some of them ate meat. They were all created as plant eaters, but apparently some acquired other habits after creation was pronounced "very good" (Genesis 1:31).

The Bible doesn't say when they gained that ability, but it does give us a clue. When Adam and Eve rebelled, God pronounced the awful curse of death on all of creation. In doing so, He not only fulfilled His promise that they would begin to die

(2:17), but evidently He actually changed (or allowed to vary) the genetic makeup of each "kind" so that all their descendants would forever be different. He changed Eve's body structure (3:16), the plants (v.18), and the animals, as well (v.14). Perhaps at this time dinosaurs and other animals acquired or began to acquire body parts designed for aggression or protection. This may be over-speculation, but sin ruins everything, and, before long, the entire planet was corrupt and "filled with violence" (6:11,12,7).

God had told Noah to bring pairs of each kind of land animal on board the Ark, including, evidently, the dinosaurs (7:15). Even though we think of dinosaurs as large, most of them were small. An average size for the dinosaurs would be about the size of a pony. Recognizing that, as reptiles, dinosaurs would have continued to grow as long as they lived, this implies that the oldest would be the largest, but there would have been plenty of room on board the Ark for younger, smaller representatives of even the giant ones. Thus, the dinosaurs on board the Ark probably would have been young adults, no bigger than a cow, perhaps.

But the world after the Flood was much different than before, with much less vegetation and a colder, harsher climate, and evidently the dinosaurs gradually died out. Perhaps they were even hunted to extinction, as would be indicated by the many legends of dragons, the descriptions of which closely resemble dinosaurs.

At any rate, Biblical history has an explanation for dinosaurs, their creation, life-style, and extinction. Christian parents are encouraged to use them to teach Biblical truth.

Recommended Resources:
Dinosaurs and the Lost World—J. Morris
What Really Happened to the Dinosaurs?—J. Morris/Ham
Dinosaurs by Design—Gish
Remarkable Record of Job—H. Morris
Dinosaurs: Those Terrible Lizards (video)—Gish
The Dinosaur Mystery Solved (video)—J. Morris

Evidence against Evolution

Is There Evidence against Evolution?

Despite the fact that evolutionists are fond of claiming that science has "proved" evolution, much evidence can be marshalled against it.

The biggest problem for evolutionists is the origin of life from nonlife. Even the simplest single-celled organism is unthinkably complex, with scores of highly sophisticated parts, all performing important functions and all mutually interdependent. The laws of statistics have convinced all who have bothered to do the calculations that even a protein molecule, consisting of a chain of hundreds of precisely arranged amino acids, could never arise by chance. And such a protein molecule is trivial compared to any of the working parts of a cell. When it is recognized that all of these parts must be present and functioning at the start, it must be admitted that life from nonlife is impossible without an intelligent designer. Actually, any living thing gives such strong evidence for design by an intelligent designer that only a willful ignoring of the data (II Peter 3:5) could lead one to assign such intricacy to chance. Every living thing, from simple bacteria to people, possesses the marvelous DNA code, which contains a library full of precise information, and without which life is impossible.

Another huge problem for evolutionists lies in the nature of the fossil record, i.e., the only physical record we have of life in the past. As is now being admitted by our evolutionary colleagues, the fossil record gives no clue that any basic type of animal has ever changed into another basic type of animal, for no in-between forms have ever been discovered. Each basic type is distinct in the modern world, as well as in the fossil record, although there is much variation within these basic types. While gradual, "Darwinian" evolution has always predicted that in-between forms would one day be found, the current rage in evolutionary circles is the concept of rapid spurts of evolution, or "punctuated equilibrium"—proposing that small isolated portions of a larger population evolved rapidly and left no fossils. But this is just a story argued from lack of evidence. Where is the evidence that things evolved at all?

Even though the gaps in the fossil record are found between each basic animal type, there are two huge gaps which should be emphasized. The evolutionary distance between single-celled organisms and the vast array of multicellular, highly complex marine invertebrates precludes even rapid evolution. In the supposedly 550-million-year-old (or so) layers of rock designated as Cambrian (the first appearance of multicelled life), sponges, clams, trilobites, sea urchins, starfish, etc., are found with no evolutionary ancestors. Evolutionists don't even have any possible ancestors to propose.

And then the gap from marine invertebrates to the vertebrate fish is likewise immense. To make matters worse for the evolutionists, fish fossils are also found in Cambrian strata. If evolution is true, fish must have evolved from something, and invertebrates must also have evolved from something. Evolution has no ancestor to propose, but the evidence exactly fits the creation model, for creation insists that each animal type was created fully formed, with no evolutionary transition.

The evidence for creation is so strong, it is illogical to believe anything else. Only a religious commitment to atheism, or a desire for the approval of those atheists who call themselves scholars, could lead one down this path. The Bible says that those who deny creation are "without excuse" (Romans 1:20).

Recommended Resources:
What Is Creation Science?—H. Morris/Parker
Scientific Creationism—H. Morris
Evolution: The Fossils Still Say No!—Gish
Origins: Creation or Evolution? (for children)—Bliss
Origin of Life—Gish
The Trilogy—Volume II—H. Morris/J. Morris
Scientific Creationism (video)—H. Morris
Introduction to Scientific Creationism (video)—H. Morris
Bible and Modern Science (video)—Gish
Gish/Doolittle Debate (video)
From a Frog to a Prince (video)

Family

A Genesis Solution for America's Failing Families?

The first institution ordained by God was the family. The health of any civilization can be measured by the strength of its families. America is sick because her families have been savaged by humanistic philosophies. Many solutions have been proposed, but only Genesis addresses with accuracy the who, what, why, when, and where of Godly family life.

Who defines the family? Humanists maintain that the family is little more than cultural convention. The Bible teaches that from the beginning God established a non-optional pattern for marriage: One man and one woman joined in covenant before God for life. Despite current debates on the validity of "same-sex marriages" and no-fault divorce, no legislature will ever change God's definition of the family.

What structure governs the family? The Book of Isaiah warns that a nation is under God's judgment when children oppress parents and women rule over men (Isaiah 3:12). In our day, the pervasive influence of modern feminism and teen rebellion are two indicators of such judgment. That God created man for the leadership role in the home is evident from the first three chapters of Genesis: Man was created first (Genesis 2:7; I Timothy 2:11–13); woman was created out of man (Genesis 2:23); woman was created for man (Genesis 2:20–22; I Corinthians 11:9); and man was held responsible for their sin (Genesis 3:1–6,9). Note also that Genesis teaches children are to be under the authority of their parents who must "command [their] children and household after [them]" (Genesis 18:19).

Why did God ordain marriage? Scripture teaches that "Where there is no vision, the people perish" (Proverbs 29:18). The same is true for families. In the Bible, "vision" refers to the proclamation of God's Word which results in clarity of purpose. The sad truth is that most marriages lack direction because they have lost the Genesis purpose for marriage. Genesis teaches that God created marriage for the perpetuation of a godly seed and the effective administration of man's dominion work on Earth (Genesis 1:28). He told them to "Be fruitful, and multiply, and replenish the earth, and subdue it." This Genesis principle is accompanied by a warning: "She (is) thy companion, and the wife of thy covenant. And did not He make one? . . . And wherefore one? That He might seek a godly seed" (Malachi 2:14,15).

When should a couple begin a family? Hollywood presents America's youth with a steady barrage of misleading messages regarding marriage. Teen-age sexuality is glorified, single-parent families are encouraged, and marriage is said to limit personal fulfillment. Consequently, many avoid marriage altogether, while others enter marriage grossly unqualified. Genesis gives us normative patterns of qualifications for marriage. **Step one:** Before a man considers marriage, he should have direction. Adam was first given a purpose and a life work, then a wife. If a man has no idea where he is going, how can he ask a woman to follow? **Step two:** Adam discovered that he needed a wife (Genesis 2:20) in his life work. The desire to better serve God with an appropriate life partner is prerequisite for godly marriage. **Step three:** The two are called together by God to co-labor in a unified dominion work for God (Genesis 1:28; I Corinthians 11:9). This work requires an appropriate division of labor. He is prepared to act as provider, protector, and spiritual leader, even as she is willing to assist him, keep the home (Titus 2:5; I Timothy 5:14), and mother children (Genesis 3:16; I Timothy 2:15).

Where can one find answers to the problems which plague America's families? Humanistic assumptions and Hollywood morality are dangerous distractions for the Christian who hopes to build a lasting family. We must "go back to Genesis" for true answers and exchange the methods of modernity for the family foundations patterned in the book of beginnings!

Recommended Resources:
The Modern Creation Trilogy—H. Morris/J. Morris
The Genesis Record—H. Morris
Christian Education for the Real World—H. Morris
The Genesis Family (video)—Ham

Human Fossils

Why Don't We Find More Human Fossils?

The fossil record abounds with the remains of past life buried in sedimentary rock deposited as sediments by moving water. If the creationist interpretation of the fossil record is basically correct, most of the fossils were deposited during the Flood of Noah's day, as "the world that then was, being overflowed with water, perished" (II Peter 3:6). These organisms were trapped and buried in ocean-bottom muds which later hardened into sedimentary rock, fossilizing the organic remains.

But where are the pre-Flood human remains? According to Scripture, the patriarchs lived long ages and had large families during their many years of childbearing potential. Where are their fossils?

To answer this, we first must rightly consider the nature of the fossil record. Over ninety-five percent of all fossils are marine creatures, such as clams, corals, trilobites—mostly invertebrates with a hard outer surface. Of the remaining five percent, most are plants. Much fewer than one percent of all fossils are land animals. This encompasses reptiles (including dinosaurs)—amphibians, mammals, birds, and humans.

Land creatures have what we call a "low-fossilization potential." As land animals die in water, they bloat, float, and come apart. It is very difficult to trap a bloated animal under water in order for it to be buried. Furthermore, scavengers readily devour both flesh and bone. Seawater and bacterial action destroy everything. The scouring ability of underwater mud flows, common during the Flood, would grind bone to powder.

Conversely, what land fossils are found were mostly laid down during the Ice Age—a land-oriented event following the Flood, which had the ability to bury animals in land-derived deposits. (And, by the way, there are human fossils in those sediments.)

But the purpose of Noah's Flood was to destroy the land communities—not preserve them—especially humans, who were engaged in sinful and violent rebellion against their Creator. God's intention was to "destroy them with the earth" (Genesis 6:13). Some creationists even postulate the pre-Flood continents were subducted down into the mantle, totally annihilating all remnants of civilization. In any scenario, what land fossils were preserved would be buried late in the Flood, near the surface, and would have been subject to erosion and destruction once again as the Flood waters rushed off the rising continents.

Furthermore, we must not overestimate the pre-Flood population by considering the long patriarchal lives and large families as typical, for "the earth (was) filled with violence" (Genesis 6:13). Bloodshed would no doubt have terminated many family lines in both humans and animals.

For purposes of discussion, let us assume 300,000,000 people died in the Flood, and that each one was preserved as a fossil evenly distributed in the sedimentary record, which consists of about 300,000,000 cubic miles. The chances of such a fossil intersecting the earth's surface, being found by someone, and then being properly and honestly identified, is vanishingly small.

On the other hand, if evolution is true, and humans have lived on Earth for three million years, many trillions have lived and died. Where are *their* fossils? This is the more vexing question.

There are as yet unanswered questions regarding creation. But in all cases, the creation model has a better explanation for the data than does the evolution model.

Recommended Resources:
Biblical Basis for Modern Science—H. Morris
Evolution: The Fossils Still Say No!—Gish
Bones of Contention—Lubenow
Dry Bones . . . and Other Fossils (for children)—G. E. and M. Parker
The Origin of Man (video)—Gish

The Geologic Column

Does the Geologic Column Prove Evolution?

Probably every textbook in use in America which in any way deals with evolutionary subjects includes a presentation of the "Geologic Column," or the "Geologic Time Scale," as it is sometimes called. This vertical display of the various geologic eras, periods, and epochs supposedly illustrates the nature of the fossil record with recent fossils on the top and older ones on the bottom.

By following the fossils from bottom to top, one can "see" evolution from simple organisms to mammals at the top. But what is the truth of the matter? Actually, the geologic column exists in only one place—in textbooks. There is no place on Earth where all these layers, with these kinds of fossils, are found *in this sequence*. The geologic column is simply a statement of evolutionary dogma, not geologic and paleontologic fact.

Now don't get me wrong. A trend does exist in the rocks which is compatible with the column. For instance, when fossils of dinosaurs and trilobites are found in the same geographic location, the dinosaurs are usually on top. But this trend is only part of the story.

First of all, in order to demonstrate evolution, there must be numerous in-between transitional forms showing one basic body style evolving into another. As has been well pointed out, we see no evidence of any major change. There are minor variations and adaptations, but no evolution!

Furthermore, each basic body style (phylum) has been present right from the start. In the lowest (i.e., oldest) level of abundant multicelled organisms (the Cambrian Period), fossils of each phylum have been found, including vertebrates! Many fossil organisms are found which have gone extinct, but no new body styles have appeared. Did evolution stop at the start?

Among the vertebrates, a case can be made for some change. Fish fossils are found in the Cambrian and people aren't. But people are vertebrates as are dinosaurs and birds. In many ways, our skeletal features are comparable to that of a fish. We're certainly a whole lot more like a fish than a coral, or a clam, or a jellyfish.

Thus, when you look at the geologic column in the textbook, you will notice that it is mainly a statement of **vertebrate** evolution, it has very little to say about the other fossil types. But it is very constructive to look at *all* the fossils and then come to a conclusion.

As it turns out, 95% of all fossils are shallow marine invertebrates, mostly shellfish. For instance, clams are found in the bottom layer, the top layer, and every layer in between. There are many different varieties of clams, but clams are in every layer and are still alive today. That's not evolution—just clams! The same could be said for corals and jellyfish and many others. Rightly understood, the fossil record documents primarily marine organisms buried in marine sediments which were catastrophically deposited on the continents, not in the ocean.

Of the 5% remaining fossils, 95% of them are algae and plant fossils (4.75% of the total). In the left over 5% of the 5%, insects and all other invertebrates make up 95% (0.2375% of the total).

All of the vertebrate fossils considered together, fish, amphibians, reptiles, birds, and mammals comprise only 0.0125% of the entire fossil record, and only 1% of these, or .000125% of the total, consist of more than a single bone! Almost all of them come from the Ice Age. Surely the vertebrate fossil record is far from complete.

Where we have a good record, *no* evolution can be seen. From the very scanty vertebrate record, an evolutionary story can be told, but the facts don't support it, and certainly don't prove it.

Recommended Resources:
The Genesis Flood—H. Morris
The Young Earth—J. Morris
Grand Canyon: Monument to Catastrophe—Austin
Mount St. Helens (video)
Search for Noah's Ark (video)
The Deluge (video)—J. Morris
A Geologist Looks at Noah's Flood (video)—J. Morris

The Ice Age

Was There Really an Ice Age?

The Ice Age has always been a problem for science. While abundant evidence has been found for continental glaciation, the cause has remained enigmatic. Scores of scenarios have been proposed: global cooling, decrease in the sun's intensity, rampant volcanic activity, etc.; but none are truly able to bring about such profound changes—none except the creation model, that is.

First, let's talk about the nature of the Ice Age and clear up various misconceptions. To start with, the Ice Age was a time when great sheets of ice built up on land. As snow accumulated in extreme northern (and southern) latitudes, its own weight packed it into ice. And then, because ice is not fully rigid, it can flow out from heavy snow accumulation areas into lower latitudes.

The glaciers never covered more than a minor portion of the globe. In North America, ice covered much of central Canada and as far south as Kansas. Weather in the rest of the world was affected, but these areas were not under ice. Some propose that there were several ice ages—from four to sixty such ages—each lasting for long periods and separated by vast ages, but the evidence for multiple glaciers is poor.

The obvious requirements for ice buildup are more snowfall and less snow melt. But how does this happen? No mere cooling scheme, shackled by the constraints of uniformitarianism can alter Earth's conditions to that extent. And, besides, if things get too cold, the air can't contain much moisture and it doesn't snow much. And so the puzzle remains.

A key to more snowfall is more evaporation, and the best way to achieve that is to have warmer oceans. We would also need somewhat warmer winters in polar latitudes to allow for more snowfall and intense weather patterns to transport the evaporated moisture from the ocean to the continents. And then we need colder summers to keep the snow from melting and allow it to accumulate over the years. Everyone agrees that these conditions would cause an ice age, but uniformitarian ideas can't allow the earth's systems to change that much. Many creationists think the Flood of Noah's day provides the key.

As the Flood ended, the oceans probably were warmer than today. The pre-Flood world had been uniformly warmer, and during the Flood, the "fountains of the great deep" (Genesis 7:11) would have added much heat, as would the tectonic readjustments late in the Flood and following it. This warmth would provide a continual pump of warm moisture into the atmosphere—thus warm, wet winters with abundant snow fall.

Furthermore, the land surface at the end of the Flood was little more than a mud slick and would have reflected solar radiation without absorbing much heat. The large temperature difference between ocean and land, coupled with strong polar cooling, would cause intense and prolonged snow storms.

Finally, the late and early post-Flood times witnessed extensive volcanism as the earth struggled to regain crustal equilibrium. This would cloud the atmosphere bouncing incoming solar radiation back into space—thus, colder summers.

More evaporation, warmer winters, more intense storms, colder summers: The result? An "Ice Age" which would last until the oceans gave up their excess heat, the volcanism lessened, and vegetation was reestablished. This likely would take less than one thousand years following the Biblical Flood.

Recommended Resources:

An Ice Age Following the Global Flood—Oard
Life in the Great Ice Age—Oard
The Weather Book—Oard
The Genesis Flood—H. Morris
A Geologist Looks at Noah's Flood (video)—J. Morris

Law and Evolution

Do Laws and Standards Evolve?

Our society has declined to the point where Christianity is excluded from the public arena, parents may kill their own fully developed nine-month baby in the womb, and the lawfulness of homosexual marriage is openly debated in state legislatures across the country. Many Christians disapprove of such practices, but when challenged to defend their position, are quickly silenced by protests to keep religion and morality out of politics.

The way in which a society addresses such controversies is directly related to its answer to the following three foundational questions: (1) Can man legislate morality? (2) If so, by what standard should man legislate? and, (3) Does this standard evolve? The answer to each of these questions is determined by one's view of origins.

Can man legislate morality? The real question is not whether man *can* legislate morality, but *which* system of morality will be legislated. All laws are either explicitly moral or procedural to a moral concept. Even laws requiring traffic lights are an imposition of morality because they presuppose the need for preserving life, protection of property, and maintaining order.

Of course, law can neither save nor sanctify. God intends civil law to be a restraint against evil, not a source of spiritual deliverance (Romans 13:4). As Creator, God has the authority to establish guidelines for right living. Ironically, it is the evolutionary humanist who argues for salvation by legislation. Because man's problems are believed to be environmental (not sin-related), the evolutionist sees government programs and better education as the cure. In such a world, the state, not Jesus Christ, is honored as man's redeemer.

By what standard should man legislate? Ultimately, there are only two standards by which man can govern: the law of God, or the will of man. Our Founding Fathers declared their allegiance to the Creator and acknowledged that He had established a law-order with transcendent moral principles: the Declaration of Independence, the Constitution, and Blackstone's *Commentaries* served as the foundation for the law and legal education in America. Blackstone wrote: "Laws . . . must rest on the eternal foundation of righteousness . . . doctrines . . . to be found only in holy scriptures. . . ."

Blackstone predicated his entire analysis of law on: (1) the superiority of special revelation (the Bible) over general revelation (nature); (2) the reality of a literal twenty-four hour, six-day Creation Week; (3) a literal Adam and a literal Fall resulting in the corruption of human reason; and (4) the Dominion Mandate of Genesis as the foundation for the law of property ownership.

Blackstone affirmed the authority of Scripture as the only legitimate foundation for society, and he specifically refuted the idea that laws could evolve as societies change.

Do laws evolve? Jesus Christ is the same yesterday, today, and forever (Hebrews 13:8). His moral law for man can never change because it reflects the immutable character of a righteous, holy God. This standard was established from the beginning and is eternally binding on all civilizations and cultures. Unfortunately, our legal system and law schools have abandoned these foundational principles, substituting a Darwinistic, man-centered concept of a flexible law modifying to fit an evolving society.

No, God's holy standards will never evolve because the Lawgiver never changes. Only armed with a Genesis foundation can the Christian answer the three critical questions and speak authoritatively to issues which define the cultural battle of our day.

Recommended Resources:
Teaching Creation Science in Public Schools—Gish
The Long War Against God—H. Morris
The Controversy—Chittick
Creation and the Schools (video)—H. Morris
The Long War against God (video)—H. Morris

Macroevolution vs. Microevolution

What's the Difference between Macroevolution and Microevolution?

There is much misinformation about these two words, and yet, understanding them is perhaps the crucial prerequisite for understanding the creation/evolution issue.

*Macro*evolution refers to major evolutionary changes over time, the origin of new types of organisms from previously existing, but different, ancestral types. Examples of this would be fish descending from an invertebrate animal, or whales descending from a land mammal. The evolutionary concept demands these bizarre changes.

*Micro*evolution refers to varieties within a given type. Change happens within a group, but the descendant is clearly of the same type as the ancestor. This might better be called variation, or adaptation, but the changes are "horizontal" in effect, not "vertical." Such changes might be accomplished by "*natural* selection," in which a trait within the present variety is selected as the best for a given set of conditions, or accomplished by "*artificial* selection," such as when dog breeders produce a new breed of dog.

The small or *micro*evolutionary changes occur by recombining existing genetic material within the group. As Gregor Mendel observed with his breeding studies on peas in the early 1800s, there are natural limits to genetic change. A population of organisms can vary only so much. What causes *macro*evolutionary change?

To yield new organs or body parts, such as are needed by *macro*evolution, new genetic information is needed. Genetic mutations produce new genetic material, but do these lead to *macro*evolution? In science, no truly useful or innovative mutations have ever been observed. The one possibility most cited is the disease, sickle-cell anemia, which provides an enhanced resistance to malaria. How could mutational changes similar to that which causes the dreadful disease of sickle-cell anemia ever produce large-scale positive change?

Evolutionists must make the basic assumption that the small, horizontal *micro*evolutionary changes (which are observed) lead to large, vertical *macro*evolutionary changes (which are never observed). This philosophical leap of faith lies at the core of evolutionary thinking.

A review of any biology textbook will include a discussion of *micro*evolutionary changes. This list will include the variety of beak shapes among the finches of the Galapagos Islands, Darwin's favorite example. Always mentioned is the peppered moth in England, a population of moths whose dominant color shifted during the Industrial Revolution when soot covered the trees. Insect populations become resistant to DDT, and germs become resistant to antibiotics. While, in each case, observed change was limited to *micro*evolution, the inference is that these minor changes can be extrapolated over many generations to *macro*evolution.

In 1980, about 150 of the world's leading evolutionary theorists gathered at the University of Chicago for a conference entitled "Macroevolution." Their task: "To consider the mechanisms that underlie the origin of species" (Lewin, *Science,* vol. 210, pp. 883–887). The conclusion? "The central question of the Chicago conference was whether the mechanisms underlying *micro*evolution can be extrapolated to explain the phenomena of *macro*evolution . . . the answer can be given as a clear, **No.**"

Thus, the scientific observations support the creation tenet that each basic type is separate and distinct from all others, and that while variation is inevitable, *macro*evolution does not and did not happen.

Recommended Resources:

Evolution: A Theory in Crisis—Denton
The Amazing Story of Creation—Gish
Creation Scientists Answer Their Critics—Gish
What Is Creation Science?—H. Morris/Parker
The Modern Creation Trilogy—H. Morris/J. Morris
The Bible and Modern Science (video)—Gish
From a Frog to a Prince (video)

Noah's Flood

Did Noah's Flood Cover the Whole Earth?

Not too long ago, a scientist who claims to believe the Bible and calls himself a creationist, came to ICR to confront us with our error of teaching a *recent* creation. He held to a five-billion-year-old earth, a view which we feel is fraught with many logical fallacies, not the least of which is the insistence that the Flood of Noah was merely a *local* flood.

Here is the issue: All advocates of the old earth insist that "proof" of such ages lies in the rocks and fossils of the earth's crust. They claim these were laid down by either slow and gradual processes, or by occasional rapid processes of local extent. The fact that many of these rock layers are of continental extent forces them to postulate migrating shorelines, widely meandering rivers, unthinkably large deltas, etc. Furthermore, the rock units in most cases were laid down by catastrophic events, but these events, they say, were rare, occurring every million years or so.

But if the Flood actually happened the way the Bible seems to describe it (i.e., a year-long, mountain-covering, world-re-structuring event), it would have laid down many layers of mud full of dead things (i.e., now rocks and fossils) covering immense areas, having been deposited under catastrophic conditions. A proper interpretation of the rocks and fossils speaks of a global, dynamic, watery catastrophe: the Biblical deluge.

Only denial of Biblical teaching could lead one to misinterpret the rocks and fossils to support long ages. If the Flood happened the way the Bible says it happened, then it laid down the rocks and fossils, and there is no remaining evidence for an old earth, or evolution, for that matter.

Let us urge you to read carefully Genesis 6–9. If God was really trying to describe a *local* flood, He certainly could have written much more clearly, for over and over again the wording demands a *global* Flood. In fact, over 100 times, the wording clearly implies a global flood. Consider these few quotes of the

many: "the face of the earth [i.e., planet]" (6:1); "end of all flesh
. . . the earth is filled with violence . . . I will destroy them with
the earth" (6:13); "destroy all flesh, wherein is the breath of
life, from under heaven, and every thing that is in the earth
shall die" (6:17); etc.

Furthermore, God promised never to send another flood like
Noah's Flood (9:11,15), but there have been many local floods,
even regional floods, since Noah's Flood. If Noah's Flood was
only a local flood, then God lied to us. Likewise, there was no
need for Noah to build an ark for his survival, for he had many
years' warning (6:3).

Perhaps more convincing is the fact that Jesus Christ based
His teaching of coming judgment on all mankind on the fact
that Noah's Flood judged all mankind (Matthew 24:36–39; Luke
17:26,27). A local flood implies a partial judgment. Likewise,
Peter based his prophecy that the existing planet will "melt with
fervent heat" (II Peter 3:10) and an entire new heaven and new
earth will be recreated (v. 13) on the historical fact of the global
flood of Noah's day (v. 6). All things considered, few doctrines
are taught as clearly in Scripture as that of the global flood.

The Christian need not distort the clear teachings of the
word of God. The testimony of the ICR scientists is this: There
is no fact of geology that cannot be interpreted by the Biblical
way of thinking in a way at least as satisfying as (usually better
than) the evolutionary, slow-and-gradual worldview.

Recommended Resources:

The Genesis Flood—H. Morris
The Young Earth—J. Morris
The World That Perished—Whitcomb
An Ice Age Caused by the Genesis Flood—Oard
Noah's Ark: A Feasibility Study—Woodmorappe
The Grand Canyon: Monument to Catastrophe—Austin
The Genesis Flood (video)—H. Morris
A Geologist Looks at the Genesis Flood (video)—J. Morris
The Deluge (video)—J. Morris
Grand Canyon: Monument to the Flood (video)

Evolution in the Public Schools

Are Public Schools Required to Teach Evolution?

There is much misinformation (or should we say *dis*information?) about this issue, so much so that there is much disparity between legality and reality. Let's take a closer look.

We must first acknowledge that teaching the scientific evidence for creation is permissible. In the most recent decision on this, the Supreme Court stated that "teaching a variety of scientific theories about the origins of humankind to school children might be validly done with the clear secular intent of enhancing the effectiveness of science instruction" (Edwards vs. Aguillard, 1987, p.14).

This decision ruled unconstitutional an effort by the Louisiana legislature to mandate the teaching of *both* evolution and creation, because the Court (wrongly) suspected a religious purpose behind the law even though this was denied, and the bill emphasized that the evidence be presented without religious content.

The Court further stated that teachers "already possess" the "flexibility . . . to supplant the present science curriculum with the presentation of theories, besides evolution, about the origin of life" (p.8). They are "free to teach any and all facets of this subject . . . all scientific theories about the origins of humankind" (p.9). The Court thus sustained the lower Court finding that "no court of which we are aware had prohibited voluntary instruction concerning purely scientific evidence that happens, incidentally, to be consistent with a religious doctrine or tenet." In short, teaching the scientific evidence which supports creation is legal!

But can it be done? In the place of freedom there exists a reign of terror by certain "civil liberties" groups and the education establishment. The word is out—any teacher who dares to step out of line can expect an immediate and costly lawsuit. Evolution must be taught as unquestioned fact. A lawsuit might result if a teacher even discusses the evidence which doesn't fit well with evolution. This evidence must be censored out of the classroom along with the abundant evidence which better supports creation than evolution. Thus, teachers are intimidated into surrendering their freedoms.

These lobby groups have, to a great degree, succeeded in convincing many that evolution is science while creation is religion. But, in doing so, they have used a bogus definition for science. Science has become synonymous with naturalism—a search for naturalistic explanations for all things—in this case, unobserved origins events in the past.

But science instruction should restrict itself to true science, that which is observable, repeatable, testable, and predictable. This would exclude both creation *and* evolution worldviews, but it wouldn't exclude the evidence. Unfortunately, the major universities continue to produce graduates who can only think along evolutionary lines. This includes teachers and bureaucrats and lawyers (who become lawmakers and judges).

There is perhaps one hope. Across America citizens are moving to reclaim schools and school boards back from the self-appointed intellectual "elite" who have too long held undue influence. A return to freedom and sanity may only stem the tide, however. Only a true revival can turn back the tide. And this can only happen as Christians and churches get back to a Biblical perspective in all areas, especially including a "Back to Genesis" perspective.

Recommended Resources:
What Is Creation Science?—H. Morris/Parker
Origin of Species Revisited—Bird
Christian Education for the Real World—H. Morris
The Trilogy—Volume II—H. Morris/J. Morris
Teaching Creation Science in the Public Schools—Gish
Amazing Story of Creation—Gish
Voyage to the Stars—Bliss
Voyage to the Planets—Bliss
A Walk through History (video)—J. Morris
When Two Worldviews Collide (video)—J. Morris

Ten Most-Asked Questions

Do the Difficult Questions Have Answers?

Throughout the years, questions have been raised regarding Christian doctrine which have caused many to stumble, or even abandon the faith altogether. Some seem rather simple, while others are difficult. But, if the Christian faith is the true faith, there must be answers, and there are, if one is willing to study and believe.

It does no good to ignore the questions, or to insist that some questions are unaskable, exhibiting a "lack of faith." If young people can't ask and receive honest, satisfying answers in their Christian homes or churches, they will probably assume there are no answers and deny the validity of Christianity. Remember, many, if not most, of the leading humanists, atheists, and anti-Christians grew up in Christian homes. A few such plaguing questions with (*very*) brief answers follow. (I recommend the ICR book, *The Bible Has the Answer*, as one excellent source of more complete answers.)

1. Evidence for a Creator God? The design and order of the universe, in particular living systems, demands an intelligent Designer. To deny the obvious signature of God in His creation is to be "without excuse" (Romans 1:20).

2. Where did God come from? The Bible reveals God as self-existent. This is a basic assumption of Christianity, but all the facts of nature support the validity of this assumption.

3. Where did Cain get his wife? Adam and Eve had "sons and daughters" (Genesis 5:4). Such unions were a genetic problem by the time of Moses, but were not a problem so soon after Creation.

4. Human color differences? Genetic studies have shown that all humans have the same color, although some have more of the skin-coloring agent than others.

5. Where did the races come from? All humans are descended from Noah's family. Isolation of language groups following the dispersion at the Tower of Babel caused certain characteristics

34

to be expressed which best fit the local environment. There is only one race, the human race.

6. What about the dinosaurs? The Bible reveals that land animals were created on Day Six of the Creation Week. There is much evidence that humans and dinosaurs lived at the same time.

7. Carbon-14? The Carbon-14 dating method is applicable only for the most recent 3,000 years or so, good for dating human archaeological remains, but not rocks and fossils.

8. Is the Earth billions of years old? Other radiometric dating schemes are thought by some to show that the earth is old, but in reality do not prove it. They merely assume great age and then work within that and other questionable assumptions. All the real *facts* fit the concept of a young earth.

9. Is there evidence for Noah's Flood? The global, mountain-covering flood described in the Bible laid down most of the world's fossil-bearing (things that died in the flood judgment) sedimentary (water-deposited) rock. To deny the Flood is to be willingly ignorant (II Peter 3:5,6).

10. Isn't Creation a side issue? Most of Christian doctrine is based on Genesis, especially the definition of, and punishment for, sin, and man's desperate need for a Savior to die in substitutionary payment for that sin. The Genesis account of creation is vital to the Christian faith.

Recommended Resources:

The Answers Book—Snelling/Ham
Science and the Bible—H. Morris
Many Infallible Proofs—H. Morris
The Bible Has the Answer—H. Morris
Gish/Aubrey Debate (video)
A Walk through History (video)—J. Morris

The Races

Where Did the Races Come From?

Waiting in airports and long airplane rides have become a way of life for the ICR staff scientist. Imagine my appreciation (JDM) when two black servicemen engaged me in a delightful conversation about the Lord one day.

As it turned out, both men were dedicated Christians, but had no previous teaching on creation, although both knew evolution had to be wrong based on the clear statements of Scripture.

Finally, they asked the question which they had always wanted to ask but had never dared to: "Where did the races come from?"

Perhaps I was reading too much into their comments, but I felt like weeping (and still feel like weeping) as I recognized what generations of racial prejudice had done to these two dear, Christian men. From Darwin on down, evolutionists have preached that the Negro race was lower on the evolutionary scale, much closer to the apes than the Caucasian. As a matter of fact, the whole concept of race is evolutionary, not Biblical, for God "hath made of one blood all nations of men" (Acts 17:26). The Bible teaches that all of mankind springs from our first parents, Adam and Eve, and then through Noah's family. Biblically, we are all sinners and need a Savior. There's certainly no difference in the things that count.

The Biblical distinction is between national groups, and especially languages, not skin color or other physical characteristics. These two men, and probably many with dark skin, had been bludgeoned by evolutionary dogma into questioning their own identity, wondering if their standing before God was equal to that of other ethnic groups.

Actually, the Biblical model regarding the origin of physical characteristics is easily the superior historical and scientific explanation. Starting with Noah's family, the creation model postulates a "racially mixed" population with much biological potential for variation. As family groups were isolated by language barriers, environmental factors allowed particular traits already present to be expressed more frequently, while genes coded for other traits were not favored and were eventually suppressed.

Genetically speaking, the differences between the various races are extremely small. All are of the same species, are interfertile, and produce fertile offspring. The most noticeable difference is in skin color, but the fact is, we are all the *same* color; some people just have a little more of that color than others. Skin shade is due to the amount of a substance called melanin in the skin; the more melanin, the darker the skin.

Brown-skinned individuals can parent children who are all the way from quite dark to quite light, or anywhere in between. But two dark-skinned parents can only yield dark-skinned children, and two fair-skinned parents can only produce fair-skinned children. Both extremes have less genetic potential to vary than those of middle-brown complexion. Both black- and white-skinned people have lost genetic information. Furthermore, the predominant shade for a well-mixed group would be brown.

While prejudice, persecution, and racial hatred follow directly from the application of evolutionary teaching, some have even proposed racism in the name of Christianity. The Christian must not allow himself or herself to think this way. The Lord Jesus certainly didn't. He was likely neither white nor black, but somewhere in between. He died to provide all men the opportunity for eternal life (II Peter 3:9, for example). Indeed, heaven will be populated by "a great multitude . . . of all nations, and kindreds, and people, and tongues (who will stand) before the throne, and before the Lamb, clothed with white robes" (Revelation 7:9), all redeemed by His blood. In the end, all racism, as well as racial distinctions, will be abolished.

Recommended Resources:
The Genesis Record—H. Morris
Biblical Basis for Modern Science—H. Morris
The Answers Book—Snelling/Ham
The Trilogy—H. Morris/J. Morris
The Origin of Man (video)—Gish
Genesis 1–11: An Overview (video)—Ham

Radioisotope Dating

Can Radioisotope Dating Be Trusted?

For decades creation scientists have shown that the answer to this question is a clear, "NO!" Its results have been shown to be inconsistent, discordant, unreliable, and frequently bizarre in any model. Creationists have, in particular, pointed out the weak assumptions on which the method is based, and the contradictory nature of its results.

A research consortium has recently convened at ICR to go further and develop a workable understanding of the radioisotope decay data from a young-earth perspective. The old-earth model doesn't work, and a better model must replace it.

However, as we look forward to a better alternative, it would behoove us to look back and restate the powerful tried and true arguments relating to the erroneous assumptions and contradictory results.

Assumption One: *The radioisotope decay rates have been constant throughout the past.* We know that some elements are unstable (radioactive), and their atoms decay and split into smaller atoms; i.e., uranium (parent) changes into lead (daughter). Since these rates of decay are now very stable, this has seemed to be a reasonable assumption. However, there are several clues that rates have changed in the past, or that some other process dominated.

For example, the existence of short half-life polonium halos in rock have been used by many to argue for rapid formation (i.e., creation) of host rocks. Even evolutionists admit that the halos are a mystery. Yet nearby, a full uranium halo might be found which would take a long period of time to form. These two "mutually-exclusive" facts convince one that something has been overlooked.

Assumption Two: *No parent or daughter material has been added to or taken from the specimen.* Changing the isotope ratio in a specimen invalidates its use in dating. However, we know of many ways in which the materials can be made mobile, most particularly through ground water leaching. But even when questionable specimens are rejected, many results are still unusable and explained away by contamination.

Furthermore, since the dynamic flood of Noah's day covered the entire globe, what rock could have escaped its effects?

Assumption Three: *No daughter material was present at the start.* Only rocks and minerals which formerly were in a hot molten condition (like lava) can be dated. But what if the original melt already had some radiogenic lead? The resulting rock would inherit a deceivingly "old" date. In recent years, the "isochron" method has been derived to differentiate between inherited material and true daughter material. Unfortunately, even this has now come into disfavor. Many "pseudo-isochrons" have now been published which yield bizarre, useless dates.

This assumption actually denies the possibility of creation, for God may have created an array of radioisotopes which, if analyzed with false assumptions, could be misinterpreted as age.

The method's unreliability is shown when rocks of known age are dated. For instance, the new (1980) lava dome at Mount St. Helens dates at up to 2.8 million years old! Such anomalous results are common.

While the method obviously doesn't work well, a better understanding of the method is still needed. To that end, pray for the new research group.

Recommended Resources:

The Young Earth—J. Morris
Grand Canyon: Monument to Catastrophe—Austin
The Answers Book—Snelling/Ham
Grand Canyon: Monument to the Flood (video)
Mount St. Helens (video)

Theories

Can Evolution Be Harmonized with Genesis?

The very first temptation came in the form of a question: "Hath God said?" Eve responded to the serpent's query by misrepresenting God's revelation (Genesis 3:3). Satan uses the same methodology today to cast doubts and undermine the Christian's confidence in God's word: "Has God *really* said that He created the world in six literal days just as described in Genesis?" Like Eve, some Christians are attempting to answer this Satanic challenge to God's word by adding to and twisting the Scriptures to accommodate philosophies and theories which are foreign to the Bible. Over the years, certain theologians and scholars have attempted to harmonize Scripture with the theory of evolution. Each attempt has failed. But no sooner are such efforts refuted from the word of God, than they are followed by some new and more innovative compromise.

Theistic Evolution: God used an evolutionary process over long ages to create.

Gap Theory: Billions of years of evolution took place in an assumed gap of time between Genesis 1:1 and 1:2.

Age-Day Theory: The days of Genesis 1 are equated with the long ages of evolutionary time.

Progressive Creationism: God created each kind of life, but did so over billions of years.

Framework Hypothesis: Genesis is an allegory only, not true history.

All of these concepts involve vast time: death on Earth before Adam's sin; the curse affecting only man's spiritual state, but not the rest of creation; the Flood was merely a local flood; etc.—all Biblically and theologically indefensible.

Each of these theories begins with at least five fatal faith assumptions, all of which are Biblically false: (1) the mind of man is fully functional and capable of knowing absolute truth apart from God's written revelation; (2) the religious neutrality of science; (3) Scripture should be interpreted in light of modern scientific theories; (4) the present is the key to the past; and, consequently, (5) gradual, uniform changes working over long periods of time as "proven" by the fossil record and the geological column.

In contrast, the creationist begins with the assumption that Scripture is its own self-authenticating witness. This means that the Bible testifies to its own accuracy on everything to which it speaks, including matters of science. While recognizing that the Bible is not a textbook on science, the orthodox Christian affirms that the Bible is a source book without which no scientific fact can be properly understood in the fullest sense. To be faithful to the text of Scripture, we must take God at His word and understand that Scripture must interpret science, not the other way around.

Man will never be able to harmonize Scripture with the assumptions of Darwinism and "Big Bang" cosmology. Every attempt to do so denigrates the word of God and undermines the gospel. Progressive Creationism and its various hybrids are not only exegetically impossible, but intellectually dishonest, not to mention scientifically flawed. In their futile effort to reconcile two mutually exclusive worldviews, proponents of these theories are demonstrating that the only thing which is really evolving is their creative ability to compromise the word of God.

Recommended Resources:

The Genesis Record—H. Morris
Modern Creation Trilogy—H. Morris/J. Morris
The Lie—Ham
Introduction to Biblical Creationism (video)—H. Morris
A Walk through History (video)—J. Morris
Genesis 1–11: An Overview (video)—Ham

Theistic Evolution

Most Christians are uncomfortable with purely naturalistic evolution. They know that creation occurred by supernatural means, not limited to natural processes. The solution for many Christians has been to adopt theistic evolution which is based on the idea that the God of the Bible employed an evolutionary process to create.

Any listing of the attributes of God would include omnipotence, omniscience, love, grace, foreknowledge, and the desire for a relationship with man. Would this kind of God have used long ages of evolutionary development to create?

Theistic evolution looks back to about four billion years ago when God brought just the right chemicals into the right order to form a single cell. This multiplied and mutated for over three billion years until He either allowed or caused them to evolve into two-celled organisms, then about 500 million years ago into marine invertebrates, such as clams, snails, trilobites, and flatworms.

Over hundreds of millions of years, many types went extinct and were never seen by man. But the flatworm begat fish, then amphibians, then reptiles and birds, then mammals. They would live and die, mutate and go extinct. Some would eat the others. All were subject to disease and starvation. Some, like the dinosaurs, also passed into oblivion before man arrived. The fossil record provides ample evidence of their existence, suffering, and extinction long ago.

Just a few million years ago there were upright-walking apes, then *Homo erectus*, and then Neandertals—"animals" who made tools, employed agriculture, utilized both religious implements and weapons, suffered from disease and malnutrition. They enjoyed music and flowers and art, but had no soul.

Then, just a few thousand years ago, God made true man. He either created man from scratch or took a subhuman animal and gave it an eternal spirit. As He finished His work, He called it all "very good." God's creation could finally recognize His grace, respond in love, and give God the glory due His name.

But was it all "very good"? Beneath Adam's feet would lay the fossils of billions of animals, many giving evidence of traumatic death. And what were the long-extinct dinosaurs? Had God been experimenting, trying to find something He could call His image? Did He not know what He wanted? Was He not powerful enough to create without so many missteps? If the creation and redemption of man was His purpose, why did He wait so long?

And why did He use the process of the extinction of the unfit to create? His very nature ultimately impelled Him, the Fit, to die for the unfit. In redemption, He would strongly denounce personal works as a method of salvation. Would He have used survival of the fittest as His method of creation and accept "glory" from His creation on this basis?

No, the righteous God revealed in Scripture would create just as described in Genesis, chapter one. Creation would be orderly and wise, with man and his walk with God the result. It would be deathless and sinless, compatible with the all-powerful, Holy, life-giving Creator's label as "very good."

Recommended Resources:

The Defender's Study Bible—H. Morris
The Genesis Record—H. Morris
The Lie: Evolution—Ham
Many Infallible Proofs—H. Morris
The Long War against God—H. Morris
The Bible and Modern Science (video)—Gish
A Walk through History (video)—J. Morris
The Genesis Record (video)—H. Morris

Belief in the Young Earth

Is Belief in the Young Earth Necessary to Be a Christian?

At our seminars and in our books, we at the Institute for Creation Research take a strong stand on the young earth. We certainly don't do this to win a popularity contest, for this position is ridiculed by both the secularists and many Christians alike. Nevertheless, we teach this without compromise and without apology.

The main reason for believing in the young earth is that the earth *is* young! The Bible tells us so, and the weight of the scientific evidence points to a young earth. While the Bible may not specify a precise date for creation, it does indicate that the earth is only a few thousand years old. Similarly, while the geologic and physical evidence cannot give a precise age, all the evidence is compatible with the young-earth doctrine with far greater evidence supporting a young earth than an old earth. There is much compelling evidence incompatible with the old-earth idea.

Furthermore, many Biblical doctrines are based on the recency of creation and the corollary doctrine, the global flood. One cannot hold the old-earth position and believe that the Flood was global, for if the Flood was global, then the entire earth's surface was altered. The Flood would leave in its wake the rock and fossil record which now is misinterpreted by geologists as evidence for an old earth. All Christians who knowledgeably advocate an old earth believe that the Flood was only local. (A few still hold the bizarre notion that the Flood was tranquil and did little geologic work. Imagine—a tranquil, worldwide flood!)

The doctrinal absurdities which result from a local flood and an old earth are well documented in creationist literature. The most serious fallacy involves the death of the vast majority of Earth's inhabitants before man appeared, and before he sinned and incurred the wages of sin. Astronomer Hugh Ross even proposes humanlike animals who buried their dead, practiced religious ceremonies, painted pictures on cave walls, etc., but did not yet possess an eternal spirit. Death of conscious life before Adam's sin implies that death is natural, not the penalty for sin. But if so, what good did the death of Jesus Christ accomplish? And what was the world like before the fall? Old-earth advocates believe it was no different from our world—with death, extinction, bloodshed, carnivorous activity, fossils.

Because of ICR's stand on this all-important issue, some have suggested that ICR teaches that belief in the young earth is necessary for salvation. This is not the case! Salvation does not imply perfect understanding of doctrine, for then no one could be saved. God grants salvation when one repents of his sin and asks for forgiveness based on Christ's death for his sin. A sinner doesn't have to know anything about the age of the earth in order to be saved.

Nor does one have to believe in the young earth to be a Christian leader. Many Christian leaders believe and do a lot of things they shouldn't. But belief in the old earth, with the implied concepts of death before sin, the world before Adam not really "very good," an inconsequential fall and curse, a local flood, etc., destroys the foundation of the gospel of Jesus Christ. Some Christians do believe in both Christianity and the old earth, but they shouldn't. Any form of old-earth thinking is inconsistent with their professed belief in the Bible.

Recommended Resources:

The Genesis Flood—H. Morris
The Young Earth—J. Morris
Grand Canyon: Monument to Catastrophe—Austin
Noah's Ark and the Ararat Adventure—J. Morris
The Lie: Evolution—Ham
The Defender's Study Bible—H. Morris
Evolution and the Wages of Sin (video)—J. Morris
Natural Selection vs. Supernatural Design (video)—J. Morris
Introduction to Biblical Creationism (video)—H. Morris

Key Bible Verses on Creation

Belief of early Christians .... Acts 4:24; 7:48–50

Body of Jesus .... Hebrews 10:5

Completed in past .... Genesis 1:31–2:3;
Hebrews 4:3,10

Confirmed by Christ .... Matthew 19:4

Corruption of .... Genesis 3:19; Romans 8:20–22;
I Corinthians 15:53

Curse on .... Genesis 3:17–20; Romans 8:20–22

Evangelism .... John 20:31; Acts 14:15–17; 17:24,25

Everlasting .... Psalm 148:3–6; Jeremiah 31:35,36

False worship .... Habakuk 2:19; Romans 1:20–25

First object of faith .... Hebrews 11:3

Foundation of gospel .... Galatians 1:8;
Revelation 14:7

God's poem .... Romans 1:20; Ephesians 2:10

God's purpose in .... Proverbs 16:4; Revelation 4:11

In six solar days .... Genesis 1:3–5, Exodus 20:8–11

Instantaneous .... Genesis 1:11; Psalm 33:6,9; 148:5;
Hebrews 11:3

Nations .... Acts 17:24–28

New .... II Corinthians 5:17

Not in vain .... Isaiah 45:18

Of man .... Genesis 1:26; I Corinthians 11:8

Of universe .... Genesis 1:1; Nehemiah 9:6; Psalm 90:2; 96:5; 104:2–5; Jeremiah 32:17; I Corinthians 15:41

Praising the Lord .... Psalm 148:3–7; 100:3–5

Recent .... Isaiah 64:4; Mark 10:6; 13:19; Luke 1:70; 11:50; Acts 3:21; Romans 1:20

Rejection of in last days .... II Peter 3:3–7

Revealing God .... Psalm 19:1–6; 65:8; Isaiah 40:12–15,26–28; John 1:9; Acts 14:15–17; Romans 1:20; 10:18

True fellowship .... Ephesians 3:9

Week, basis of weekly calendar .... Genesis 2:1–3; Exodus 20:11

Wisdom .... Proverbs 8:22–31